CATS WILL BE CATS

CATS WILL BE CATS

Felipe Galindo

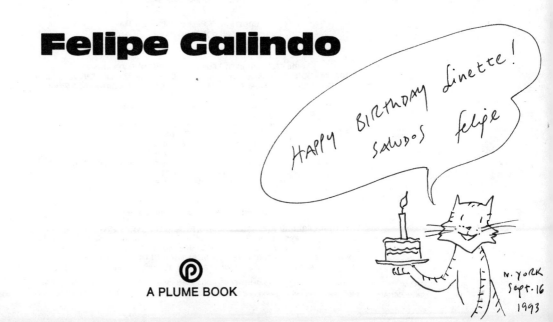

HAPPY BIRTHDAY Linette!
SALUDOS Felipe

N. YORK
Sept. 16
1993

℗

A PLUME BOOK

PLUME
Published by the Penguin Group
Penguin Books USA Inc., 375 Hudson Street, New York, New York 10014, U.S.A.
Penguin Books Ltd, 27 Wrights Lane, London W8 5TZ, England
Penguin Books Australia Ltd, Ringwood, Victoria, Australia
Penguin Books Canada Ltd, 10 Alcorn Avenue, Toronto, Ontario, Canada M4V 3B2
Penguin Books (N.Z.) Ltd, 182–190 Wairau Road, Auckland 10, New Zealand

Penguin Books Ltd, Registered Offices: Harmondsworth, Middlesex, England

First Published by Plume, an imprint of
New American Library, a division of Penguin Books USA Inc.

First Printing, June, 1993
10 9 8 7 6 5 4 3 2 1

Feggo means *Felipe Galindo Gomez.*

Some cartoons in this collection appeared previously in:
the *New York Times, Mas Magazine, Cats, Cats, Cats, The Cat-Cartoon-A-Day Calendar, Stupid Jokes for Kids* and *Nexos & La Jornada* (Mexico City).

 REGISTERED TRADEMARK—MARCA REGISTRADA

LIBRARY OF CONGRESS CATALOGING-IN-PUBLICATION DATA
Galindo, Felipe.
Cats will be cats / Felipe Galindo.
ISBN 0-452-27062-6
1. Cats—Caricatures and cartoons.   2. American wit and humor.
Pictorial.   I. Title.
NC1429.G19A4   1993
741.5'973—dc20   92-44550
                                                          CIP

Printed in the United States of America

BOOKS ARE AVAILABLE AT QUANTITY DISCOUNTS WHEN USED TO PROMOTE PRODUCTS OR SERVICES.
FOR INFORMATION PLEASE WRITE TO PREMIUM MARKETING DIVISION, PENGUIN BOOKS USA INC., 375 HUDSON STREET, NEW YORK, NEW YORK 10014.

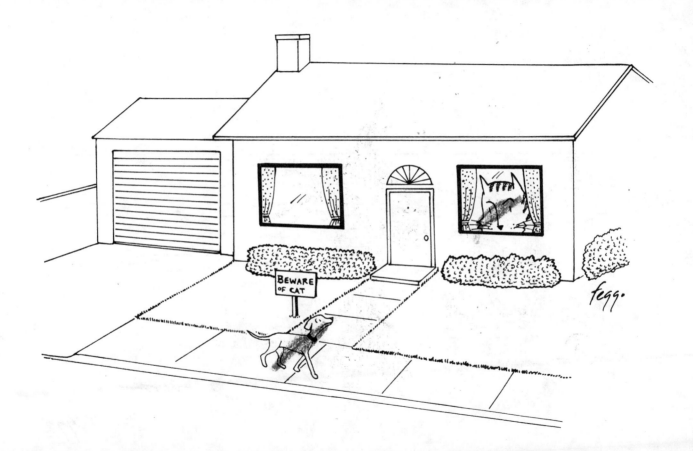

FOUR LIVES TO GO

Say "Meow."

Looks like you have a surprise for me.

They are in charge of doing cirrus clouds.

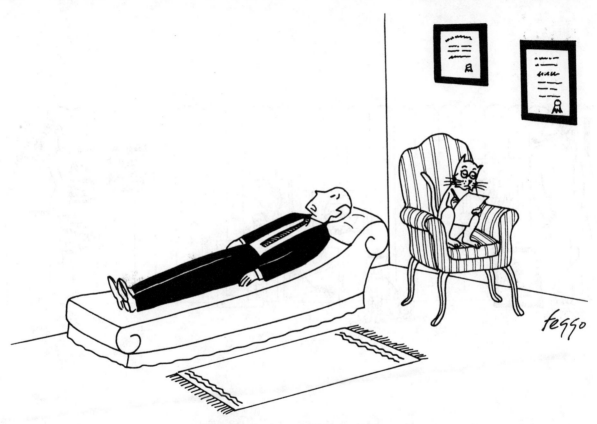

Everybody treats me like a mouse.

She was napping in my bowling ball bag.

feggo

Please don't shoot!

This species dominates Planet Earth.

I want to be kissed by a princess.

Now he uses a spray can to mark his territory.

Of course it's catfood cake, it's *her* birthday!

What kind of engine does she have? American or Japanese?

To insure your cat you need nine policies.

I don't see the fun in this.

It's happy hour, you get two for the price of one!

Quick!! Change our bets!!

This one is for kitty.

I was Cleopatra's cat in a previous life.

feggo

I don't believe you are Persian, let me see your passport!

Do you want me to call the fire department?

Wait, I have a better idea!

And what do you think you're doing?

HOFFMAN, GOLDFARB, ZUCKER & Tabby

Try to land on all fours.

We have a portrait of the serial killer.

I'm sorry, but pets are not allowed, son.

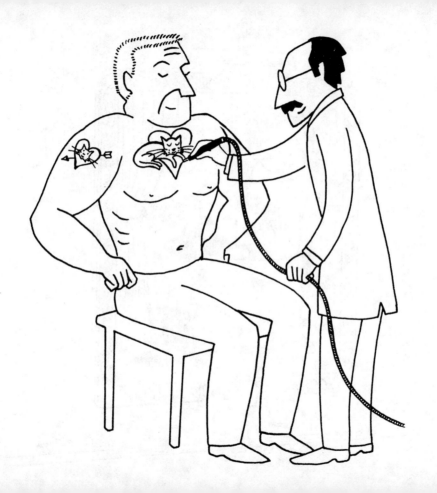

What do you mean the cat wants out?

She doesn't trust labels.

feggo

PUSS-IN-SNEAKERS

feggo

Would you mind with that purr? I'm trying to do my job down here.

Sorry, but you won't get more if we plant him.

Would you have tuna-scented cards? It's my cat's birthday.

Don't you dare!

You don't have to wash those plates, Mom,
she already cleaned them up.

And this is my bonzai cat.

Mom! Wait!

May I suggest you bring in more than a couple of mice?

Are you sure Japanese cats only eat sushi?
This is becoming very expensive.

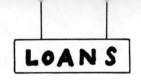

I'm afraid your kitty is not enough collateral
to lend you money.

Bruno is not content with catnip anymore.

Now you want a tattoo??

I guess it's time to cancel our Cat-of-the-Month club membership.

Oh-oh, there goes our honeymoon!

Ferguson, this is not exactly what I had in mind.

He sprayed the king's throne.

Do you know you are also a fish? Your birthday is March 9.
Therefore you are a *Pisces*!

It's the only problem with my cat's hair toupee.

Give me a mean look!

When I find a new star, I'm going to name it after you.

About the Author

**Felipe Galindo is a free-lance cartoonist and illustrator
whose cartoons regularly appear in the
New York Times and other publications. *Cats Will Be Cats*
is his first cartoon collection.**